nothing out there

nothing out there

poems
by
Paul B. Roth

Vida Publishing, Inc. Glyndon, Maryland 21071-0296
1996

ACKNOWLEDGEMENTS

The author is grateful to the editors and staff of the following publications in which many of these poems first appeared:

Black Moon
The Glass Cherry
The Higginsville Reader
Waterway
The Bitter Oleander
Yefief
The Rippling Waters

For information address Vida Publishing, Inc., PO Box 296, Glyndon, Maryland 21071-0296

Library of Congress Catalog Card Number: 96-60530

Roth, Paul B., 1949--
Nothing Out There: poems / Paul B. Roth

I. Title
811' .54
ISBN: 0-9632547-6-6
First Edition

For my father Joseph Roth

CONTENTS

Part Three

Speech From Silence, Gain From Loss: The Poetry Of Paul Roth

In a time when clamor exudes from fantasies, cacophony bursts from empty abstractions and a type of babble emerges from the deadness of what is termed "lived language," colloquial mimesis and its impossible representation, Roth creates a poetic language through the incarnation of the divine in the real, through the fusion of the external and internal, the self and the butterfly, the self and the rain, the self and the cat, to suffuse an envelope of silence that separates from the noise of the false, the fashionable surrogates for reality.

Through his poetry, Paul Roth brings a silence into the world, but it is a silence that speaks, a speaking silence, one that puts a hitherto unheard language into our blood to flow to every part of our body and to flow out of our body, overcoming personal limitation to grow arms that embrace what was once the outside --- hearing the speech of Roth's silence, his naturalistic and this-wordly mysticism, our transformed selves caress the cardinal, the worm, the leaf *ad infinitum*, and in turn we are caressed by the cardinal, the worm, the leaf *ad infinitum*. Finally, we are the cardinal, the worm, the leaf that is no longer the cardinal, the worm, the leaf that existed when the subject and object were separated, but now a new substance, a new substantial reality.

There is a love in Paul Roth's poems, a love that whispers and can only be heard by our inner lives.

Paul Roth's poems are linguistic rituals to exorcise the false values of society and the voice of the self-alienated who has been spoken by others, not speaking a self, an incommensurable self, the self of darkness that is light. Roth's poems cleanse the consciousness of human lies and construct a superconsciousness. This exorcism is a very important element in Roth's poetry. Exorcism is necessary if we are to be more than puppets of a puppet master who does not exist, to be victims of a language that in its popular usage only speaks lies and alienation. Roth overcomes the evils of the public order of language, rescues us from the fallen state of language, restores us to a linguistic garden of Eden.

Paul Roth developed from The Immanentists, a group of poets that included Alan Britt, Silvia Scheibli, Steve Barfield and originated in Tampa, Florida. Accounts of this school can be found primarily in Hugh Fox's *The Living Underground* and *The Immanentist Anthology: Art Of The Superconscious* (New York: Smith, 1973).

Duane Locke
Tampa, Florida
July 22, 1996

Part One......

The smoke is now making the first sky of the year.

---- Issa

Old Heart

You were the quiet one
who came from another language
who taught us
to pray for the burning man
to keep him holy
to feel in his chest a broken and slowed fish
flap through a sea of six million tears
and touch wood where once there was flesh
words where once there was a mouth
and all the yawning abyssinian cats
that sat in red cushioned rattan chairs
watching everything final
float toward the Tiberian dusk
are not listening to the wild notes of the saxophone
leaping off the bannisters of the veranda
are not noticing the psychiatric kleenex
drifting down among black stones in a silver sea
but are instead licking the tears off your quiet hands
as they carry among the warm clothes
in woven baskets on your swaying brown hips
the washed and folded night

Losing My Father

Now that you are perfectly still
and your cold ashen body
your lighter head
that I'm the last to embrace
the last to kiss once more
can no longer be reached by the moon
or the shadows it attracts
when the wind stands still
I realize
that the great silence
in this very room
mirrors my tears
and that for all the time
you ever lived
and for even the short time
you are now dead
I won't now or ever
like so many others
miss your presence
as much as I will miss listening
to that other silence
always coming to me
from all sides as a child
and having
as you were always the first to say
no real voice
to speak of

Status Quo

I stand close to basically
the same place
waiting for that caress of constellational light
except for tonight
when so much snow blows over my face
wets my lips
and looking up at my study window
I see sleeping
behind vertical blinds
my cat Dreamer
whose eyes closing over
a car's red tailights
place their all but hidden illumination
quickly into a dark rabbit hole
the same way I might absentmindedly remember
an old friend like the delicatessen owner
who is now dead many years
but about which it is said
he gave up his life in pursuit of serious music
in order to earn a living
submerging cornbeefs into deep steaming pots
right up to the swollen
red elbows and broken wrists of his guitar

A 4 Part Innervation

Red pear leaves
lure yellowjackets as close
as my pencil to this page

            *   *   *   *

Filling hollow rock
the melting water a rabbit drinks
before running off

            *   *   *   *

Spreading wood ashes
over the soil with the sounds from my rake
ends summer

            *   *   *   *

Growing square around the red brick walk
moss softens
the barefeet of falling leaves

Confessions Of A Silence

1

For a long time I had looked for a quiet place, even though this looking came to little use. There were I'm sure better days when I could have laid with my hands behind my head in the cool shadows of deep grasses. Better nights when I was brightened by the hidden sides of stars. I still remember their reflections gathering in dew formed at the tips of those long grasses. I still remember seeing myself in those reflections and how distinctly I was actually someone else. It was the first time I knew what my life was like to another living it. It was then that I started to love the sound of falling snow on dry leaves. Can you imagine I never knew that? And sometimes signals came as if from a nostalgia of the quiet place I was seeking; where beneath the imprints of broken, muddy twigs, there was a flow of water under snow soaked leaves near a pond's edge. It's a struggle to know how to keep myself a secret.

2

I'm bringing the word up. I'm breaking the surface of the page and darkening this little space for a long time. I'm making room in the blankness. I'm stretching it wide enough so as not to tear or injure its air of whiteness. You should know that this is my work. I have faced the page many times and been stricken by its emptiness. I've turned it every which way only to find it always stays the same. I've noticed, however, how the mark of one letter on it changes it forever; how it becomes upright, develops a spine and grows vocal chords! It not only learns to speak the letter and the word eventually engulfing it, but takes on the appearance of an object no longer a void. Now I know its significance, even when it has lived beneath the bones of its whiteness and during absences of blemish. I know too whether it's enhanced by a word printed correctly or diminished by one crumpled up inside the wastepaper of ultimately having to speak to myself out loud.

3

In a moment, I'll tell you why I'm afraid of everything. At night, I go out and gather as much warmth as possible from the earth's dark nests, holes and burrows. Inside broken shells, wrapped around bark stripped twigs and in the dark regurgitated grasses, I stay warm laying at the entrances to homes I know I can never again enter. I don't even have my own home anymore. I've quite simply become the man who sits alone or walks around by himself. I'm sure you've seen me. Just another stranger not saying much and not anywhere considered to be one of the regulars. Will death someday taste just like my silence? After all, everything else in my life was, by others, pretty well defined. My hunt had become nothing more than the vague accomplishment of going to work in the lead smelter. My fresh kill, no more than a cashed paycheck. In fact, it only gave me the power to go to a nightclub where the music accompanying a topless dancer was distastefully steadied by the rapid heartbeats of young boys who sink beyond recognition into the streets of Rio de Janeiro. Young boys who, in their desperation, day after day, shoot muddy gutter water into their phosphorescent veins. Who do anything to escape the starvation that's their life; the poverty instead of paid bills and a lovelessness forever: life's new high.

4

I'll always love this: this dark room, this single light off above the table, this silence on the edge. Here I'll write everything down to the very last word. I'll speak with the soft spoken fingers of a wind that slips through the cracks below my window's sill. Like always, my writing will sit me still to the task at hand. I won't move very much at all. I'll only be able to want, on one hand, what the other hand contradicts. I'll only be able to recollect the inkless and graphite deficient nights of my much younger and longer days. Days when I'd given away too much darkness; when I was taught so many ways to avoid it, to eat it up, to dissolve it so completely with fear; to crowd it out with candlelit dinners, campfires, reading lamps, map lights and television sets. I'm afraid that I'll someday forget that my childhood was always measured by how much silence I really enjoyed; by how many days without it were unbearable. How many days my dreams had to steal from me for the sole purpose of creating a surplus of not so many more long nights.

5

My mosaic grey and white cat sleeps in the easychair. I'm reading a suspect book about the recent past on board a boat sailing over a corpse and blood stuffed river in South America. (Espero que sueños con los angelitos). For a moment, I look up from under the once green water where the mouths of the dead are the color of the rust blossoming around the torn bumperstickers on submerged cars. I hear only a lack of syncopation among my many clocks. The hours of available air quickly leave. I forget how to hold off the water's disappearance any longer. Years ago, as a boy, I remember a warm rain fell and filled my empty hands. Pale yellow roots and pale green leaves had dug in through my fingernails and sprouted from the backs of my hands. I wore no rings back then as I husked and dry mixed white bowl fulls of Indian corn. I could see from my longhouse, looking out across a white field, a black tree standing with no shadow in the snow. I realized then that I might never see it reach up to the pupils of a wide-eyed moon. Beneath my eyelids an unseen dream was taking place. And there, in that dream, turning the corner with his collar turned up, a hurried stranger was rushing to my door. His knocks counting out the unaccountable feathers as they were dropped from formation by migrations of thick geese. Hidden deep inside my study, deep amongst books about the last people to have ever read books, his knocks, like carhorns, jumped in my blood. Not afraid to answer the door, I was simply putting a pencil to the rest of this writing in my life.

6

I grew up admiring the cement encrusted red brick school building, and did so without the ritual of a cigarette played out in its corners. I did it without any choice of abstaining from what was so easily perscribed as remedies by all night pharmacies. Now, I'm finally who I am yet mostly who I was not meant to be. I finally grew tired of balancing prime numbers, equations without equivalence and theoretical conclusions to memorized questions never clearly defined to begin with. Now I'm mostly afraid of not being heard debating against the plan to expand the square footage of a superstore closer to where fur, wings and claws which never hurt anyone begin. Beginnings driven from their homes in black pickup trucks while it's still dark and others sleep. Speeding over roads of crushed shells, leaving far behind those who go on fighting merely to survive the safety-off on the child held and loaded rifle. The child standing guard at the front door to his wounded mother's home.

7

After many years I'm writing to you again. It's amazing that I've avoided what's most obvious in my life. Even when I try hard to close up and push out of sight all the torments of my disappointment, all the rage at my easy willingness to withdraw to a supposed place of refuge, I've ended up being nauseated either by a commonplace phrase or worse, a routine kneeling in the worship of some perverse rock'n roll. I end up writing to tell you that all I ever really did was look for you everywhere. I started the search in the dark centers of white bean flowers as they striped the seeds in green-gold sunflowers. I kept looking around the perfect heads of purple alliums. I was told I'd find you under thick red apple orchards, fogged-in vineyards, slippery stone paths, wet streets and down long brick alleyways in this humid city. And I expected most to find you past the front door to the parlor and in the aromas from your kitchen, your closets, your bathrooms and finally up the steps from your basement through both dreamed and sleepless nights alone or shared. Laying here in your bedroom without you, I wanted once again to listen with you to that endlessly slow Cambodian music. I wanted to hear it filter through the rain that breaks up the flowering in black cherry trees and drops it over the bleeding forehead belonging to someone else. Someone who never heard the bells or the solemn waters in the falling rain as we now do. Someone who never again got the chance to stand ready, but who stumbled and stretched out along the waste of our pain on this table at which we sit, our hands folded, our legs crossed, as if we were finally having a life of our own.

8

Many years later I woke up. My voice, pale blue and surrounded by white stone became imperceptable and spoke only in fragments of letters hard to hear. It came suddenly from an aloneness which rapidly changed its clothes from news broadcasts, political categorizations and call-in talk radio shows, and put on instead the spotted skin of a tree frog as it slipped into a wet darkness. There, between brown pond water and a log fallen long ago across the green pond where I was standing, I was anxious and distressed about this absence, this lack of the familiar, this presence of the forest and the pond, this treasure of all that's been lost to me over the years, finally being left in the hands of so many unsuspecting strangers. Strangers who would eventually embarass me, calling me by my real name and knowing full well I'd have to pay attention, have to obey their command. Is there enough wind to hold me up and deliver me from where all things meant to be, but never are, exist? I can't go on talking about where it's always the last non-repeatable second of time, the catching of my breath, the laying back against stones in a black wall of sky and at the last sighting of wind, for the first time ever, knowing what was facing me at my very own end.

9

I live the still life. When you try and find me, I become your absence. Where you're not, I am. I even live your death forever. Let go of me when you fall off to sleep at night and I'll rise from the edge of your bed where you give up the breathing that sleep requires. You appear in my dreams but you never fully recognize me. I'm the dark one you miss looking at. No.... I'm not actually hiding, but you don't know me as well as I know your absence. I'm able to see you where and when nothing else exists. You're the one who's afraid to wake up and for whom sleep has become the enemy. Even though it once had the ability to heal all your dreams, all your sickness, all your hope, it now seems not to be trusted. Has every frequency we know in each other been driven into the same static as our car radio, deep into the dark canyons? When your eyes open and close like they do, their tears, although rare, are they still a glad and welcome sadness?

10

Today I'm letting go. There are many who'll try to hold me back and keep me from leaving, from ever again seeing crushed beer cans tossed from car windows in a bored weekender's dream. I'm sorry that I can't help but tell them I can't stay. Among so many others I see a woman in whom I once stayed long enough to sow a field right through another summer of red poppies and grey rain. A woman the color of whose lipstick I saw on the filter of a cigarette discarded by the side of the road. Now I find it hard not to notice that its red resists fading into the bright cardinal's flight through dark green arborvitae. And to think I once knew this woman's name, although it was admittedly a long time ago when I lived as a known person. Anyway it doesn't really matter now that no one wishes to recognize or even speak to me anymore. Yet subsequently what little they leave me to say, I've pretty much learned to keep to myself. I guess I'm looking for ways to save my voice for the rest of this life; to keep it filled on long walks with footsteps, green silence and a dislodged stone in whose hole I should lay down just once and curl up in the same position as water will after the next heavy rain. What little of the sun is left, reflects off the rearview mirrors of passing cars and falls into the splashed pieces of a deep puddle. The puddle's undertow pulls me back against the darker side of my blood while uneven numbers of birds are counted out in full against a soft wall of wind and blue sky. The side is filled until I know I'm finally ready to bring this wall to the edge of my own darkness. Until I'm thrilled that the wetness on maple leaves, seen after a heavy rain, is saving up to be the same type as my blood.

11

I'm seen running across the boulevards and down the dark entrance ways to the Metro. I'm seen struggling with the soft hydraulics closing its doors. Passengers on departing cars use my misfortune, my giving chase, to talk with one another for no other reason than to hide their own loneliness. Much the same way they let the television special, or the admission paid to kiss the hem on the traveling guru's purple robe, hide the dark purple claws, the brown-grey feathers, the turning white head of the chicken hawk in flight across a cold window of sky opened to the bottom of their dried and hidden blood. They never notice me walking through shopping malls against the processional of their one endless face. Their look is of hope that the happiness supposedly purchased with more rounds of ammunition at the sporting goods store will be used first thing the very next morning to hunt the chicken hawk. Each of them tries to tell me that precisely at dawn, the air will be surprised and the murder retrieved by a trained dog. All week long the dog's been tied up in a cramped backyard, left with nothing else to do but gnaw at the rectangular expanse of his chain link fence. Each of them tries convincing me that the blood on my hands is from gripping the leash too tight around this dog's neck and even though that fails to convince me, they insist that the hold my empty hand has on the steering wheel, while driving at high speeds across the interstates, is all the proof they need to refute my belief that the fist n'existe pas.

12

I start letting everything pass me by. Whatever is handed to me, I simply put off to one side. I prefer to watch my hands fill up with light and the songs that the spread of their fingers sing while holding each other against a cold wind. I know this doesn't exactly make it any easier to know who I am. Sometimes I'm the spot no one sees the sun hitting deep inside the forest; that black-gold gash of light across the unscarred birch. Sometimes I'm a dance of lights without partners or ripples on a deep green pond. I wonder now if I'll ever be able to assemble out of straw, out of oil spots lifted off black asphalt, the unknown name of a blood dried wind, the name of a white-tailed brown bird folded in my hands as a child when I sat for hours at our kitchen table. I remember my legs dangling, not touching the floor my parents reminded me often that they owned and had paid for in full. Across the street, in the house opposite mine, our neighbor was thrusting his arm into a flowering bush and pulling out a few branches filled with white blossoms. Not hearing the screams from the bush he presented to his delighted wife the bloodless bouquet.

13

     I know that things hidden from us either jump stone walls, scurry quickly into deep holes, or hop behind thick leaves to an unseen perch. I've watched them slip into dark water and hoof it through tall grasses around the edge of my night. I've seen the sun flicker when a winged insect veered away from my face just in time. My hands and my eyes always seemed useless in finding any trace of it. Eventually I just had to take the time to lay down on my back and breathe the out in. I pressed my head hard against the earth and meditated the water of roots and stones. In this position, time gradually buried my head. It's voice never avoided being the buzz of flies in the torn stomach of a carstruck raccoon. In fact, I'm told it went all the way to its last turn-around, remaining, just like everything else, hidden from us.

Stone Wall On Woodchuck Hill Road (After Tu Fu)

Wild yellow cucumber flowers
stay open in the moonlight.
Water runs over a rock ledge to the herb garden.
Its sound thickens as it hits
the orange beds of dropped pine needles.
Clouds fill in the colors of a rainbow around the moon.
I smell rain from a long way off.
A small cc motorcycle breaks the silence.
I try getting back the voice
I once heard the wind give my garden bells.
Tonight maybe a cooler breeze
will wake up in the damp pine needles.
If I should hear my voice in them
it'll most likely be speaking
in the chatter of that furry black squirrel
who runs the length of this stone wall
like a single wave at sea.

After A Music We Both Try To Hear   (for Gordon Moore)

As soon as everything else is gone
and all I hear
is your thumb tapping
the rubbed wood of your guitar
I'm going to offer you
my other hand
that writes
and does not play
in trade
if you'll just stand still with me
in this blue depot of sky
and feel against your back
as I do
a future generation
pushing
trying hard to get through us
trying to originate
the way
sunflowers blossom their seeds
from our full faces of summer
the way spiders emerge from warm dirt
trapped under your stone fingernails
the way my nervous system
deposits seeds in places
only the wind can reach
and only the sharpened sides
of a black-capped chicadee's beak
can crack open

The Unheard Silence

Every chance I get
I put my hands over my mouth
I keep very quiet
listening all the time
for the sound of wings
climbing higher in the sky
and it's a moment well spent
as long as I'm really listening
and not just hearing
what some TV documentary
stretched out over many nights
wants me to hear
as long as I'm really listening
to mosquitos
gnats and yellowjackets
that aren't passed up
aren't avoided
or pushed into the background
as if they never sting
the hand-held camera
as if they never
buzz inside a microphone
as it's picking up other sounds
that everyone else around them misses
because their footsteps
underwater
in an unmapped stream
are just way too loud

Family Vacation

Hidden in the shadow
I leave on this
and other hotel white walls
that someone always later
replaces with his own
are secrets even I do not know
am never given
enough time to find out
or at the very least
no one ever tells me how to hear these secrets
how to leave myself in their place
each time I go outside
where the sun turns my transparent shadow
in circles that form spiderwebs
and flexes them in and out
according to how much
the wind is blowing behind my eyes
where I think all my memories
are stored
until I finally fall asleep
in my parent's speeding car
and in my dreaming
enter the crease
that's left behind
by the pitched axe
in my father's
or is it my mother's
smile

Young Woman At A Picnic In The Rain

The lightning flash
off the brown shoulders in your white dress
against the dark background of the crowded pavilion
catches my eye
and overlooking your face
overlooking your low-cut breasts
and your silkless legs
instead
I'm watching your long hands at rest with each other
as if folded inside the low shadows of mushooms
as if hung in small dark waterdrops under oak leaves
beneath a rock ledge where you once lived
until it all makes me feel very old
standing here against the shine of your brown skin
which I know I'd enjoy pressing between my fingers
but cannot
knowing that would make you invisible
and that I'd lose forever
the one woman
who just by standing still
who just by looking
over the heads of every other man in the place
might somehow see me
waving my arms as I do
from the path on which she's now standing
and down which I must crawl
every night of my life
as long as her look
is unable to light my own way

After Holding A Handful Of Mud From The Montezuma
Wildlife Refuge

Today I'm not going to let myself
be deceived by the automated leaves
that fulfill the four seasons
in rotation within the living rooms of those houses
that are surrounded by fences
made of stone that's mined from a collapsed mountain
made of wood that's hewn from trees whose stumps
now pop their cold heads up
just above the brown neck of this swamp water
and call out with no mouths
to anyone who will listen
that this will be the last time they speak
that these words will never be repeated
no matter if our hands should turn to rain
or our eyes to sunlight
because for so long we held onto ax handles
and toggle switches
that turned on bandsaws and planers
that turned on visions of wealth
of treeless forests
full of underground roots
that we were all politically convinced
were still very much alive
by virtue of the fact
(if you can start to believe that contradiction)
that the striped lines
in shopping mall parking lots
were the perfect reflection
of their cleanly decapitated beauty

So As Never To Forget

After many days
the absence is noticeable
because the trees
the wind in the trees
and the seeds in the wind in the trees
are not there
and not only that
they're not even missed all at once
but more gradually
like water drying up around a drainplug
and when they're finally noticed
taken in for questioning
for days on end in police stations
shackled and handcuffed
and then boxcarred to camps designed to make infinite
so much momentous flesh
their smoke rises up
to a sky that rolls over in pain
revealing a darkness of stars on its back
and looking so badly scarred
it's as if the sun
could hardly help the night stay put
could ever let it be
what's burning
with the same eyes
we like to call
meaning
without ever having to use
its few chosen words

The Last Things

The monotone poet
I heard early this morning on *National Public Radio*
was given an award for identifying all of the last things
the last things
about which everyone knows
but for which only he's now given credit for knowing
the last things
that stay not because survival imbues them
but because survival denies them the luxury of death
the last things
that belong to those who are hand in hand
whose lips press against other lips
whose body fluids deposit one into another
and who listen for the other to finally be gone
since it doesn't matter anymore
whether one stays attached to the other or not
beyond the protrusions of their flesh
that have always linked them inseparably
I suppose from the very beginning
in spite of what so many men say their god said
to that first man and that first woman
lost in the archetype of the same day
in which all the trash of their accumulated wealth
was picked up
and the rotting of an apple from an unpicked tree
smelled to both of them
newborn

Part Two....

Well... my life has taught me to be more curious than
afraid.

--- Ishi

The Ch'an Cycle

Ch'an # 1

Every turn of the path
I see the same arrangements of flowers.

Clematis, phlox, black-eyed susan, wild tulip
all dig in along the path.

I step carefully
so as not to sever any unseen vines.

Behind me a stream pulls its voice
off the rocks it is smoothing.

A cardinal's red hints of sunset.

Left as is
I walk happily home.

Ch'an # 2

The falling snow makes me an old man.

White hair and beard
I am grandfather of the snow.

My dog no longer knows my gentle hand on his head.
He growls at what he doesn't know.

Inside when we melt
recognition and licking will be alike.

Ch'an # 3

In twilight.

Music comes
from the home with the open door.

Smoke from the burning of leaves
gives me an appetite.

With no shoes and a torn shirt
I am glad
the night is warm for sleeping.

Ch'an # 4

I go every morning to the stream
to drink.

When I carry my cup
the birds don't know who I am.

Empty-handed
they are so happy to see me.

Their fast shadows
are the pulse I feel in my blood.

The cup of water on my wood table
fills with bird dropped seeds.

Ch'an # 5

I have no candle and I sit alone
all night with my poem book in the dark room.

I write in it only new words.

Inside I hear the padding of cat paws
across my wood floor.

Outside green pines behind a falling snow.
Grey rocks buried.
Clear streams cutting through a snowbank.

I look down at my face full of stones in the water.
Leaves and broken branches at the bottom of my silence.

I'm never speaking my own language again.

Ch'an # 6

It is cold.

I stamp the snow from my boots on the stone entrance.
My cat barely lifts up his head.

The distance from my door to the cooking fire
misses your company.

Wood I bring inside
tries to sing of its days as an inhuman forest.

I listen without you listening.

Days before
our bodies were covered with kisses and the first snow.

Now the distant but lenitive
fingers of your absence have taken over.

Ch'an # 7

The house is no longer quiet.

Drums and strings
handclaps and dancing shake the floorboards.

I put my hands over my ears like this
to protect the silence.

In the distance
I can no longer hear so many leaves falling.

It's true their sound and my silence
exist without a mouth.

Ch'an # 8

I look back
after my walk in deep snow ends.

Where have I been
only the snow and I seem to know.

It's easy to find where I live
if the wind has not blown my bell clapper off.

My friend who visits me each year at this time
says it's getting harder to find me.

I say the way is the snow filling in my footprints.

Ch'an # 9

I hear your voice from a long way off.

Bees in red peonies
and orange bordered moth wings
rubbing the glass of my lamp
keep me attentive.

I hear in their voices
some of the words I can't understand in yours.

When I see you again
I promise not to ask what you said.

Ch'an # 10

The horse in the pasture is shifting its weight.
Snow on his back.

Overhead
shadows of crows drop down in his eyes.

The horse looks down
sees blue star shaped flowers
clustered on the buried shoulders of dead generals.

Yet even in their graves the horse is afraid to eat.

I leave his saddle draped over the wood stall railing
one more day.

Ch'an # 11

I sit at the back of the house.
My fingers still burning from being in the cold so long.

I melt ice to drink and boil for cooking.
It takes a long time between the warmth of my hands.

What I end up tasting are only your dreams
wherever you awake.

You ask if I've eaten.

Ch'an # 12

I sit here on my own.

Your poem arrives on horseback.
It took days to find me.

When I read it
I throw back my head and laugh.

Years ago when I came to this place
and you would not follow
I took many pens and no paper.

Now I will use the back of your poem.

Ch'an # 13

Everyday I have less to say.

Hands that cover my mouth
are shadows of the branches on bright snow.

Where I stood at the window this morning
my cat is now licking his fur.

Outside sounds from the chopping of wood
mean no crow shadows crossing over my table.

Ch'an # 14

I know the path I'm walking everyday
not by counting its stones.

Some say
one million is not much more than one.

Down the mountain
there are even men who will argue
with anyone who says zero has no value.

I live poor up here.
If a stone is no longer in its place
I try to go where it's gone.

If I can find it I'm lost.

Ch'an # 15

Life is short;
take
your time.

Ch'an # 16

I sit by an overturned rock whose wet side dries.

The wind blows a scrap of paper my way.
I bring it inside.
My black and white cat sleeps on it.

I write around his white paws.
I keep my erasures in the path of his swishing tail.

When I get up from the table
waiting for the ink to dry
his spread paws have smudged
what no language ever said.

I try writing all day and come up with nothing
but his mouth rubbing down against the paper's edge.

Ch'an # 17

I sweep light snow from the path.

It's dark shape
curving out of sight against the snow's edge.

When the last shadows are gone
I come inside.

Your footsteps are easier to forget
if they leave by this path.

But now that you are gone
I can only look the other way.

Ch'an # 18

I clean my house before each journey.

I walk down the mountain in the morning.
I cross many streams feeding a shallow blue lake.

The raft I pole across is at no cost.
If it's not on my side I may wait for days.

Closer to the village I hear the sound of icicles dripping
drowned out by small plane noise.

I'm already missing
the small birds who feed on crumbs outside my door.

Will they be waiting when I come home?

Ch'an # 19

I wake up and stay in bed.

I watch steam rise off the warm snow
on the sill of my south window.

The house has no sounds.

Last night
half a moon was in the pine tree.

I never saw the other half fall off.

Ch'an # 20

Since it is winter
there is more time for everything.

Wood stacked in piles between two pine trees
is home to the spiders.

When I am cold I build a small fire.
I need just enough heat for brewing echinacea tea.

Using any more wood would only leave
these spiders homeless.

Ch'an # 21

I come home from a town meeting
many asked me to attend.

My advice it seems was critical
in the way they made their decision.

I was asked if the forest edge near the mountain
getting less and less anyway
was really necessary.

I surprised them with a little deer I held out in my hand.
Creasing my palms in its blood was a dried up river.

When I asked
no one was willing to tell me when
our next meeting was.

Ch'an # 22

I love the quiet.
Somedays I have as much as I want.

Nearby ice is melting.

It drips quickly but freezes
in my hands cupped to catch and drink it.

I am no vessel.

Ch'an # 23

My friend is coming up the mountain.
From a long way off I can see his cold breath.

His flat backpack and walking stick,
his worn bowl and bare hands are all he has.

On his way I'm sure he sees
the ice caused breaks in maple tree branches.

He is coming to celebrate the end of winter.
Traditionally we like to sit and eat warm oranges.

Orange juice dripping in the snow
is the blood of our tears.

Until then
I'll just keep sweeping the path.

Part Three....

Just be willing to die over and over again.

--- Suzuki Roshi

Distance

How far away you are
while I'm undoing knots in the dark.

The smell of you
falls in raindrops on my palms.

Here all the faces of the day look the same.
Here yours has no match.

Your lips and the glass
from which you rarely drink
never seem empty.

Sandgrains asleep
beneath the smudge of your fingerprints
try not to show it.

Blind Attraction (for Georgina)

I find you where nothing else stands up
against the wind.

This wind having fast steps down a snow packed rock trail
below the mist above a frozen waterfall.

In a place where your footprints always lead away.

Where there's a silence
in the voice I no longer want you to speak.

Where lightning flashes
its shadows of blue ice through a heavy falling snow.

Where I keep one of these shadows for myself
should someone ever ask me your name.

Winter's End

There's so much afternoon to cover
and the snow deepens.

Late winter
and the light is slowly a little longer.

I think of you letting go
holding your hands in front of your face
in prayer over the lasting light.

Nothing ever moves on its own.

At your side
the white prayer shawl folded in a square
neatly and parallel to the bench front
slips to the ground unnoticed.

When asked your name
weightless letters that fall limp in the shawl's silk
are picking it up off the floor for you.

In A Name

All afternoon
the lengths of shadows drape long grey rocks underwater.

I am coming in off the blue lake.

Brought from a long way off this red boat
is at capacity.

Children who accompany me
sing a guessing song to try and learn my name.

They sing long after I've walked off.

Morning Of The First

I'm out walking early this morning.

I cross a stream in shallow water and rest here by it's edge
leaning with my stick against cold rock.

Maroon dragonflies skimming the surface of this stream
never ripple it a bit.

Sunlight is pleated in the rainbows of their wings.

A bell moving back and forth in the wind
without ringing.

Forgotten Lover

When you speak
you pronounce the clouds
the raindrops and the darkness without a sound.

Your silence makes my name more than it is.

The only words I wish to speak to you now
have no meaning in our language as we know it.

I tell you in writing what I could tell myself
but would feel left out should I suddenly speak it out loud.

You see your face
in the river water you drink from your own hands.

Tell me whose face in that waterfall behind you is that?

Equinox

I put my hands together and I stop talking.

A green song awakens
from a budding of leaves at the height of a red cardinal's call.

I prepare the room I swept out this morning.

All around my face
the air is black and yellow with butterflies.

I breathe.
I breathe and I blow on a small fire.

Dry leaves fly up above the stone wall.

After Drinking All Night With Old Friends

I walk along grey cliffs above a black lake.
My hands are empty.

Earlier I saw roadside crows pecking grain out of gravel.
My shadow changed their color.

I am not as sure-footed as my youth once was.
I'd like to rest with the snow in fallen branch piles nearby.

Sudden flight startles me.

Hard To Say

I rest my walking stick against the wood door
and sit down inside to write.

The rain has its own words whose diction
my language confounds.

When I say rain
too many drops fall that can be heard all at once.

When I stop trying
the nearby stream takes over my words
and closes my mouth.

Ice gives way near the stream's edge where I step.

Hard To Write

I sleep little.

The cold keeps me awake
and my poems stammer their lines out of shyness.

When my friends visit and stay overnight
not one among them notices the way I am smiling.

It will be hard but I will try one day to write it
into one of my poems.

You see my words are the same as these callouses
from the axe I carry in one hand or the other everyday.

Spring At Hand

Wood bundled under my arm
I walk the black gravel path along the canal.

Long grasses matted at the canal's sides
are pale brown and not green.

I hurry up so tonight I can smell my own fire.

I notice the echoes of crows
rising up from the stubble of corn at dusk.

Each one the beginning of an oak leaf I remember
so many summers ago.

How You Are

I'm quiet all day
letting the white of my writing paper do all of my breathing.

I sit very straight at my wood table.

I listen for the inner hum
that comes from the lowest notes in your piano.

Not surprising that what I don't have any name for
sings out in your voice.

Understand when we are this close I must lower my eyes.

Trash Day

I wake up.

A cool breeze hangs at the open door
where I'm sitting.

I half close my eyes
and the darkness and the light are almost the same.

I save up on unused letters
whose words that might differ in language
never will in sound.

Gradually my skin will fall off the bone,
and my blood dripping to earth
will have a chance of reaching a nearby stream.

Someday when I put my hands into this stream
instead of their long fingers
thin fish will swim out kicking up silt
from the green and brown algae bottom behind them.

I learn to throw less and less away.

Green Bell

A green bell rings in the morning.

I go to the open window
and stand naked against the heat and sweat.

My only movement
is to sit down as straight as I can.

All day my breathing lengthens the bell's ring
until it's only one sound.

At dusk the sun at my back as it vanishes
wakes me up.

No one's seen me.

Birthday Poem

A chair rubs against the wood floor.

Someone in another room is standing up
and shuffles out.

I sit alone behind an open door
and think this is the darkness and the silence I have sought.

When I look outside I am still completely blind.

I do not see
the shadows that follow the day into this room.

I do not see them
fill in the legs of spiders who soften with their webs
this corner of darkness where I sit.

How they breathe uninterrupted for me!

A Longer Distance

Stay where you are
when the night reaches its arms
wrapped in my warm skin around you.

Stay where you are
keeping clear the forest path
that I may one day walk in darkness to your door.

Stay where you are
blinded under lemon trees by a sea turning salt so sour
it tastes like a windless sail.

Stay where you are
licking at the origin of iron and coal
the smelter's black hands with a fire and flux covered blood.

Stay where you are
if you no longer know where I am.

Practice

It's raining early this morning.

Pulling grubs and worms out of spring grass are blackbirds
I do not bother by sitting still.

Thin incense smoke spills little by little into the air.

From my room feet first I go stand in deep river currents
and stop pushing the unwanted away.

Later the water I carry up the mountain
loses the moon where the pail's bottom has broken through.

I've given up nothing.

In The Air Above A Mountain Range In Oregon

Up here my life vanishes.

Snows are swept up the sides of these mountains
by winds who are the only knowers of my name.

Unknown to me
I call out in a white voice
that searches the echoes of snowflakes
falling between green and blue spruce branches.

Even if I never know my name
at least the tininess of my white voice will have
this body of snow as its echo.

Your Blue Door (For Silvia Scheibli)

When your blue door opens
stones with holes of wind fill your face.

You open this blue to the bottom of the sky
and make the lasting light of stars
that once was dead
the color of your ageless eyes.

Roses open from your skin
and green ice plants flowering violet
push your lips above the surface of the sand
that with your thoughts you made
a refuge for the waves.

Sandpipers leave tracks in bracelets
around your long arms that are sandbars
holding the underwater shadows of cypress trees
you said were much too dark for nests.

Now you sleep with broken shells at your feet
and the willet's beak
curves down into the flesh of your dreams.

Foam on your lips speaks the silence.

Nothing Out There

Nothing out there
can keep me from the overgrown path home.

The coo of the morning dove
reflecting off my face in this rock filled stream
is beautiful but cannot hold me.

Only the night that closes my eyes
where there's no sleep
and a darkness full of hands
that was the gift of strangers
cares to greet and comfort me.

Out in the open
I hold everything else that I fear.

Since I'm always my greatest unknown
even I do not know it.

The Light On The Wall
(Arcosanti: 1984)

I am faraway on the earth.

Alone below a rough ceiling
I sit very low in an adobe home.

I want to rise with the light on the wall.
I want to leave only my shadow behind.

I want your reach to my hand
to hold only that shape made by the wall's end.

Now what is beneath my skin
no longer struggling against me
replaces my touch on stone with this light on the wall.

How I love this light on the wall.

The way branches here keep from tangling
with the shadows of my arms.

How I love the heat of its silhouette
in my face.

Its ripples from my open mouth
the only trace of my breathing.

Samsara Reversed

I hold onto the recipe of my fathers:
the one that fills the empty bowl,
the one that holds the empty bowl,
the one that is the empty bowl.

When I am hungry
the empty bowl fills me with hope.

When I am full
the empty bowl fills me with humility.

When I am sad
I do not fill the empty bowl with my tears.

When I am happy
I do not try and drink away these tears.

When my heart becomes this empty bowl
my breathing will go on forever.

The Storm, Your Voice

Your voice
is the sound of wood
moving in the woodpile.

Your laugh flames up
in a small fire
I build in my memory.

Dead
you are a new moon
at which frogs on this darkgreen pond whistle.

In my upstretched hands
a little moonlight connects one finger to the next.

I have instead of a hand
one full day.

In The Way

My skin is in the way.

It wants to split open
to mix its blood with the sweet water that gorges cherries
that inflates the transparencies of grapes
and stuffs every plum to its ripeness.

It wants to mix its bone with seed.

It wants its rebirth
its new breath to have flickered
in the vertical leaf blades of yuccas
quivering in the breeze.

It hangs from my hands at my sides.
It shapes my breathing.

I want to be just as alive as the ripened fruit
inside whose skin my blood takes up a liquid residence.

I want no end to this death.

Getting There

At night I witness the flight of fireflies
through the pine trees.

Wind shaking cold raindrops
from pine needles
over my sunburned shoulders.

I bending
over my garden in the dark.

The earth
moving under my feet
on the backs of red earthworms.

My toes digging in
holding on.

How Many Lives Do I Miss

How many lives do I miss that are mine?

How many voices exchanged for stones
rubbing against each other's skin beneath the earth?

How many hands broken open by the wind?

Can I expect anyone
to rescue me from the oblivion of day?

Am I left looking where tall pines pierce sharp grey clouds
and darken their green with the sunset?

Do I try and take this darkness to my lips
knowing if I speak up no one will hear me anyway?

Am I any more accurate writing every soundless word?

Staying In Touch

Between the many greens of leaves
and raindrops,
the shadows that birds after flying off
leave in the pine trees,
I lose your face.

I used to think it was the wind.

I also believed that pine needles, cones and bark
dropped into this wind
covered your words in the voices of birds.

After many years I lost touch with you altogether.

Even the stain of red geraniums on your fingertips
that left a trail on everything you touched
was gradually dissolved by rainfall into the earth.

Seeds underwater in a rock hollow stood still in the wind.

Each time I thought we'd get in touch once again,
there was the light of stars
and a moonless sky on this water.

Hot Afternoon In The Outward Life

There's little chance for us in the heat of the day.

Somewhere ice cubes break apart
and rise clinking against each other
to the top of a water glass.

Here we press the deep clay in our hands
over our mouths
and drink.

A taste like blood fills our mouths.

When we speak
only the wounds of words are what we hear.

We've swallowed these wounds for so long
that even when we repeat what we hear
we're told again and again
there's no such thing.

Composition

I keep to myself.
There are hands I can do nothing about.

My face is never the same.

Stones at my feet know a song
none of my music can accompany.

I listen
and in my sleep
compose.

Catching Up

My hands unfolded in my lap
palms up
nest in the silence
meditated by hens on their eggs.

Fragile air
in our future we will pay to breathe
comes so easily to us now.

I exhale at your death
where I know you can't wait.

Dim Recollection

I forget everything.

Your name is the movement of branches
after crows take off.

Your face is the stillness
and your voice ceases to sound anymore
where others speak.

Forgive me
if we've been introduced.

In Hiding

I hid longer than was necessary.
It took years to find me.

I held out for as long as possible.

When they finally found me,
tall dogs commanded by black dressed men
strained at their leashes,
their testicles swinging,
their salivation lavish.

If I only knew their names.

Stillness

Dark ice
clings to the roots of trees
standing in shallow water.

I reach but cannot reach its edge.

I want to grip and feel it
melt against my knuckles and palms.

Its sound
the numb pain in my hands
where I write this.

Paul Roth lives with his wife and three sons in upstate New York where he is both editor and publisher of The Bitter Oleander: A Magazine of Comtemporary International Poetry. A 1974 graduate of Goddard College in Vermont, his other poem titles include *After The Grape* (1969; UT Review Press); *Basements of Tears* (1973; Ann Arbor Review Press); and *Half-Said* (1977; The Bitter Oleander Press).